The Little Book on Giving

The Little Book on Giving

GAIN IT ALL BY GIVING IT ALL

by

Lucien A. Stephenson CKA®

Copyright © 2015 Lucien A. Stephenson CKA®
First Edition, Revised

Illustrations: Primie Villa Querobin Parcon – General Santos City, Philippines

All rights reserved. This book and any portion thereof
may not be reproduced or used in any manner whatsoever without the express written
permission of the publisher, except for the use of brief quotations in a book review.
Printed in the United States of America.

Scripture quoted by permission. All scripture quotations, unless otherwise indicated,
are taken from the NET Bible® copyright ©1996-2006 by Biblical Studies Press,
L.L.C. All rights reserved.

ISBN-13: (Custom) 9780692364451
ISBN-10: 0692364455
Library of Congress Control Number: 2015900415
The Little Book on Giving, Dover, OH

Table of Contents

	Acknowledgements	vii
	About the Author	ix
	Introduction	xi
Chapter 1	It Will Take Planning	1
Chapter 2	All about Abundance	6
Chapter 3	Gifting Insurance	14
Chapter 4	Increasing Tax Efficiency	18
Chapter 5	Outright Gifts, Giving Cash	20
Chapter 6	Asset-Based Giving	24
Chapter 7	Beneficiary Designation	28
Chapter 8	Private Non-Operating Foundation	30
Chapter 9	Donor Advised Fund	33
Chapter 10	Structuring Charitable Giving Vehicles	38
Chapter 11	A Charitable Remainder Trust	45
Chapter 12	Wealth Replacement Trust with a CRT	51
Chapter 13	What Strategy is the Best Strategy?	54
Chapter 14	Conclusion	58
Chapter 15	Summary of Strategies	62
	Appendix A	65
	References	67
	Endnotes	69

Acknowledgements

I ESPECIALLY WANT TO THANK my wife, Chinyere, for her contribution to this project and her continued support. As is the meaning of her name, she is truly a "gift from God."

I dedicate this book to my daughter, Adora, and to my son, Kelechi. I want to remind them that they can do anything that they set their hearts on!

About the Author

THE CALL TO FAITHFUL STEWARDSHIP from Luke 12:35 is this – "*Get dressed for service and keep your lamps burning.*"

Lucien A. Stephenson has been in the financial services industry for 18 years. He holds a Six Sigma Green Belt from Villanova University and has an Executive Certificate in Financial Planning from The Ohio State University Max M. Fisher College of Business. Lucien is a proud member of Kingdom Advisors. He is Certified Kingdom Advisor™ (CKA®), an independent Registered Investment Advisor (RIA), and an independent, fee-based wealth manager dedicated to exceeding the expectations of his clients.

As a Certified Kingdom Advisor™, Lucien has the experience and capability to deliver Socially Responsible Investing (SRI) as well as Biblically Responsible Investing (BRI) strategies for his clients. He is trained in the Paterson Center's StratOp process with which he advises churches, non-profits, educational institutions and social service groups in strategic and operational planning.

As President and Chief Compliance Officer for Stephenson & Company, he is responsible for the firm's strategic vision and clarity when placing investment assets.

Lucien has authored a book on this subject, '*Total Clarity*™ – *Understanding the Four Keys to Successful Investing.*'

Contact Lucien at:

Phone: 1-330-232-9199
Email: lucien@stephensoncompany.com
Stephenson and Company Website: http://www.stephenson-company.com/

Kingdom Advisors Website: https://www.kingdomadvisors.com

Introduction

1 Timothy 6:17, 18 – *"Command those who are rich in this world's goods not to be haughty or to set their hope on riches, which are uncertain, but on God who richly provides us with all things for our enjoyment. Tell them to do good, to be rich in good deeds, to be generous givers, sharing with others."*

"We don't get credit for what we leave, we get credit for what we give."
~Andy Stanley, Senior Pastor, North Point Community Church

Do you realize that, in many cases, people spend 40 years accumulating wealth, 20 years trying to preserve it, and about 40 minutes deciding how it will be dispensed when they are gone? I know people who spend longer than that to plan a one-week vacation trip!

I wrote this book to provide easy ideas and give you strategies that can be described as "strategic charitable giving." They are seriously effective in helping you integrate your faith into your financial and estate planning and all your giving. You will need one or more professionals to help you set them up, but the time and the results are well worth it in many, many ways.

My intention is not simply to provide motivation, but to explain the actual tools and vehicles that exist today to do such strategic giving. These are practical strategies you can choose from for your giving that will allow you to gain a benefit here on earth and ultimately hear "Well done!" by your Heavenly Father.

The question that this book will help you answer is simply:

"Would you be open to paying <u>zero estate tax</u> *to the government by giving it to charity instead – if it would not materially impact the amount you are able to leave your children?"*

If yes, then this book will provide the tools to accomplish your desire to give.

This book will allow any individual or family to work with a well-qualified financial advisor, CPA or attorney for fast implementation of a plan of action for giving to charity. After reading this book, you will have the background and information to become a generous giver. All you will need to do is name the strategies or tools of interest to you, and have the advisor see how one or more of them fits into your current situation. Based on that analysis, you can make an informed decision.

One of the approaches I have been using more and more often for my clients who are in organizations such as churches or non-profit corporations, educational institutions, social services enterprise is the **StratOp Process**. The word "StratOp" blends two words vital to a successful strategic planning process. "*Strat*" stands for strategic, the art of planning for tomorrow, today. "*Op*" stands for operational, the discipline of managing today, today. I am a certified facilitator of the StratOp process and I have been trained to take an entire team whether a church, non-profit or family office through a six phase planning process in which you gain perspective on where you are now and what is needed to get you to breakthrough. We start with ***perspective*** - where are we now; ***planning*** - where are we headed; ***action*** - what's important now; ***structure*** - what form is needed for success; ***management*** – how are we doing; ***renewal*** – what must change. The whole process is built upon the financial – because both today and tomorrow must be strategically financed for a long-term success.

Being "a generous giver" does not mean that you should give in a haphazard way! In fact, the strategies outlined in this book will show you (or, as the case may be, you and a number of other family members) how to give even more than you suspected you could, with a few straightforward operational steps to take.

These are indeed the same strategies and tools already implemented by some of America's wealthiest families. My goal for this book is that it will become a quick reference guide for high capacity and high net worth (HNW) donors who are planning your charitable giving. This guide can help you increase the size or frequency of your donor gifts by introducing strategies, tools and techniques that are not common knowledge. In essence, your family will soon be more strategic and proactive in your giving. You will have a clear plan.

Remember that a well-informed CPA, attorney or financial advisor can be a good resource for initial advice on giving, and for providing timely advice on various concepts with regard to charitable giving.

If the advisor is a Certified Kingdom Advisor™ (CKA®), so much the better. A potential danger to strategic Kingdom giving is that you may have surrounded yourself with financial advisors, accountants, CPAs and attorneys who do not share your same core spiritual values or convictions – and that can be an impediment to reaching your true giving potential. I suggest that you go online to the Kingdom Advisors website to search for attorneys, CPAs or Registered Investment Advisors (RIA) who share your Christian spiritual values. Find those who have completed the Kingdom Advisors Core Curriculum. You will find resources and websites at the end of this book. I am convinced that any advisor who cannot add his faith to his practice should consider quitting the financial services business – unless he does not come in direct contact with any saints in the course of his work.

Gifts to charities are, as we all know, tax deductible because they are defined as serving the public interest. Gifts to charities will also allow you to hear, "Well done, good and faithful steward," when that gift serves Kingdom purposes.

I simply want to help you who seek ways to prioritize God in your giving. As you read this book, you will discover it goes beyond just your tithing at church, and into much more generous giving.

> Luke 16:11 – *"If then you haven't been trustworthy in handling worldly wealth, who will entrust you with the true riches?"*

Let's look at some ways to handle your worldly wealth, such that your Father says, "Well done, good and faithful servant."

CHAPTER 1

It Will Take Planning

I ONCE HEARD SOMEONE SAY, the "ultimate objective as stewards of God's Property is to do with it what the Owner wants us as managers to do with it."

With proper estate and tax planning, which can include charitable trusts and other charitable entities, you can be the ultimate steward of God's property and minimize the amount of taxes you pay year after year and when you leave this earth. Giving can pinpoint many opportunities to take care of yourself and your family members and still continue to support the ministries and charities you are passionate about helping as part of your complete estate plan.

There are many ways that you can give to charity or a ministry. Tithing is not the only way to give to your local church!

You can make gifts anytime during your lifetime, or upon death only. You can make gifts directly, or use a vehicle for the gift.

If you plan to make substantial gifts, you can establish a trust or a private foundation (although there are many lower-cost options), create a community foundation or a Donor Advised

Fund. Even if you have already created one or more of these vehicles, keep reading!

Giving should be a family affair – and if it has not been so before, it can become one now for your family and its future generations. Giving can provide you great personal satisfaction, but the ultimate goal is to hear, "Well done, good and faithful servant."

Yes, you know that giving can also give you a current tax deduction; it can reduce your tax liability year after year if that is a goal. Giving can even allow you to avoid paying capital gains tax and reduce the amount of taxes on your estate when you finally leave this earth. We all know this. What we need to learn is how to give back, pay forward and be a Kingdom steward in the process.

In the U.S., it is primarily high net worth families and high net worth individuals who do most of the giving and gifting. Although churches spend much of their time urging their congregation to give a tenth of their income, many studies have shown that only 3-5% of church-goers tithe or give a tenth of their income! Thus, almost every church in America has just one or two families that provide the majority of the financial resources that the local congregation needs to complete its mission. This book can give you ways to contribute to your church's mission and prosperity that go beyond and around tithing.

DATA ON GIVING
A 2011 Bank of America Study of High Net Worth Philanthropy indicated that about 95% of HNW givers give to charity versus

65% of the general population. Other studies show that giving as a percentage of HNW household income was about 8.7% and the average amount donated by HNW households was around $52,770 per year.

Give Differently
Charitable giving can play an important role in many estate plans, and it is not only you as steward who benefit.

My point in this book is that you can do it *differently*. That charitable gifts lower net taxable income, which can also lower overall tax rate is no secret. Let's just do it better, more efficiently and satisfy Kingdom directives as we do so.

The Bible has more than 2,250 verses that deal with money, wealth and possessions! Contrast that to only about 500 verses that deal with heaven and hell combined. So, what could this mean? I think it means that God is very concerned about your responses to and actions around the wealth of this material, human world with which He has blessed you!

Will you use your abundance for Kingdom gains or hoard it away? Your earthly wealth is in direct competition with God for rulership of your life. As an example, we know that God can heal our bodies of all ailments. But if we believe instead in our wealth, what do we do? We use our wealth to go and get the best healing or care at the best medical facilities from the best doctors anywhere in the world. In this scenario, you deny that you have any need for God. Healing from God or healing from men? That is the competition God sees in us created by our worldly wealth.

In his book *'Fields of Gold'*, Andy Stanley said, "Giving was simple when I was a child. From an early age, I was taught to take one dime out of every dollar I received and put it in the offering plate. I never knew anything else." He was raised to believe that giving was just one of the things you did with money. It was effortless. He goes on to say, "And since I wasn't really earning the money anyway, I never felt any fear associated with giving. I certainly wasn't concerned that giving away money might be a threat to my quality of life. I always had plenty to eat and clothes to wear." He continues, "Over the years, as my income increased, I began to notice a slight hesitancy in my giving. I was still giving a dime out of every dollar. But now it was adding up to hundreds or thousands of dollars at a time." He began to feel the tension of really giving.

Perhaps you had a similar experience as you grew up. This is another sort of competition God sees created by our wealth.

You will not feel pressured, after reading this book, to give your weekly tithe to a ministry, because you will have set up a way to give that is both different and perhaps more generous than your tithe amount was. When the offering plate comes around, you might get awful stares for a while, but you will not care. You will already have given through a charitable vehicle that you control. The words, "I have to think about it" or "Let me pray about it" will not have to come out of your mouth. Although it may sound spiritual to state, "I will pray about it," you may never remember to pray.

> 2 Corinthians 9:6 – *"The person who sows sparingly will also reap sparingly, and the person who sows generously will also reap generously."*

Even the IRS allows you to deduct 100% of your gift up to 50% of your adjusted gross income (AGI) each year, if you have used it to gift cash to a registered charitable entity of your choice. You even receive a deduction for up to 100% of your gift up to 30% of your adjusted gross income for gifts of cash given to a private foundation. So, on earth as in heaven, you have a choice: You can hoard money away and not give at all, or you can give wisely and receive a blessing in heaven and here on earth. When you hoard, you may just be letting the government have it all by default as taxes. By sharing wisely and generously, you may take the government out of your wealth picture entirely.

As a sidebar, I said 50% per year, but you can actually give more than half of your AGI in a year. The IRS allows a donor giving cash to a public charity to *deduct* up to that 50% limit in one year, yes. However, the excess over 50% can be *carried forward* and may be deducted over the next five years. (See IRS reg. 1.170A-10). Your giving need never interfere with the cash flow you need for your normal living expenses.

CHAPTER 2

All about Abundance

> Psalm 72:16 – *"May there be an abundance of grain in the earth; on the tops of the mountains may it sway! May its fruit trees flourish like the forests of Lebanon! May its crops be as abundant as the grass of the earth!"*

WHEREVER WE ARE ON THE planet, we are surrounded by the Lord's abundance. Even in the most astonishing corners of the world!

For you who already have an abundance and want to be obedient to Christ in giving, and who desire to experience the joy of giving, I provide you a clear Kingdom-based strategic plan for giving.

This book is also for those of you who understand that if you do not assign portions of your accumulated wealth today, the wealth you believe to be yours will be taxed away…and no one you love, no organization you are passionate about, no private cause that needs your support will ever benefit. The government will do as it wishes with the wealth collected from you and/or your estate. I believe it is better to have a say in how your abundance is shared!

You must be aware that there are many ways to give, be it to family, a bona fide charity or a ministry. You can:

- Make a cash gift outright
- Use a trust for transfer of assets
- Name a charity as a beneficiary in your will
- Gift non-cash assets like your interest in a business or your ownership share of real property
- Designate a single registered charitable organization as beneficiary of your entire retirement plan or life insurance policy
- Designate more than one beneficiary, who share in the proceeds of your retirement plan or life insurance policy

There are individuals who could write a check for a million dollars, but it takes a different type of courage – and a different kind of mindset – to gift 10% of your business to a charity! There are strategies that will allow you to give to charity, in both cash and non-cash gifting, and still leave an inheritance for your heirs.

Any giver with a strategic Kingdom plan for giving can avoid capital gains taxes.

EXAMPLE: Every $100 of capital appreciation given by you avoids $15-$23 in taxes depending on your tax bracket. As a percentage saved, that is significant! Most people simply choose to sell the asset and pay the capital gains tax or give it to charity. It may be more beneficial from an income tax standpoint to gift the asset to charity and have the charity liquidate or sell the asset.

PHILANTHROPY

There has always been generous, world-changing philanthropy conceived and carried out (or at least funded) by the wealthiest of our American families. The Mellon's are a family that stand out as one of America's billion-dollar dynasties according to a Forbes list of America's wealthiest families. In fact, only the Du Pont family has had a longer run. The Mellon's have maintained a $12 billion fortune, the 19th-largest family net worth in America, one greater than the Rockefeller and Kennedy fortunes combined. They've done this quietly. Most of the Mellon's are very happy "being under the radar," according to a descendant of Thomas Mellon, who himself owns a barge company in Pittsburgh, Pennsylvania.

Thomas Mellon was born to farmers in 1813 and immigrated to America with his parents in 1818. He settled in western Pennsylvania. Thomas Mellon had a philosophy about money. He thought that making money came with the expectation that each generation leave a bigger pile of wealth than he or she started with. While all the branches of the family and their businesses operate independently, they've almost universally employed smart tricks that protect and increase core capital, minimize taxes, including setting up generation-skipping trusts and making charitable contributions in stock. But the real secret boils down to a family ethos that values one thing over all others: capital preservation and its growth over generations.

> Proverbs 13:22 – *"A benevolent person leaves an inheritance for his grandchildren, but the wealth of a sinner is stored up for the righteous."*

You should no longer find yourself giving *reactively* after learning some Kingdom-founded strategies; you will already have the tools just like the Mellon's and the Du Pont's for generous, planned, proactive giving.

We have to understand that we don't have to cut into or in any way reduce our personal costs of living and expenses to give.

While sacrificial giving is wonderful and a God-honoring act of faith, there are other ways to multiply the impact of your giving!

Context

While I encourage everyone to have a strategy for lifetime charitable and philanthropic giving, we must keep in mind the legislative and economic context that is always evolving. Governments are in charge of taxation and other policies to keep our economies on an even keel, and the resultant legislation is not always 1) easily understood for those of us interested in preserving our personal and business wealth or 2) conducive to giving in the way we used to do it. I give two examples here to demonstrate how this can be so – one of which is current, the other historic. Both deal with recession contexts.

My first example is one that many believe we are still in the midst of experiencing. Governments around the world – from the US to South Korea to the Netherlands – enacted a wide range of fiscal and monetary 'stimulus' policies starting in 2008, in a belief they were turning the recession around. These have included austerity measures (remember Greece), tax cuts and rebates (China in 2010; Germany in 2009; the George Bush administration in 2008) and government spending plans (deficit spending as in Hungary; infrastructure rebuilding projects in most nations, increases in social welfare programs or payments – mostly from 2008-2012), as a result of the 2008 'Great Recession' as well. This is what governments do.[1] That it affected many individuals' wealth and the demise of many a business is a matter of record. That it affected many families' philanthropy is less discussed.

As my second example, I turn to US history. During Herbert Hoover's presidency, the nation's economy took a serious dive into recession, as has been well documented. From 1929 to 1933, the GNP deteriorated from $103B to $55B. Those with any work were earning half as much as before the crash, such that purchasing power vanished. Unemployment rose from its former healthy 3 percent to over 25 percent. Government officials acted to turn the tide. Representative Christian William Ramseyer of Iowa was instrumental in seeking and enacting monetary reform legislation in the 1931-32[2]. As one Congressman contended in discussions of some aspects of this reform: "After allowing the big boys to play with their money during their lifetime and after allowing them the pleasure and pride of piling up dollar on dollar while living, a generous estate tax should be levied on their death."[3] The federal government ultimately passed laws in 1932 requiring all high net-worth (HNW) American families to donate a considerable portion of their families' wealth to the general welfare of this country.4 This is how governments redistribute wealth.

How can we know the effects on our own circumstances until the dust settles? That is why I say that context is important to understand. Very few HNW families know that the federal government gives you a choice – in spite of appearances to the contrary and when all is said and done – in *how* you support the general welfare of the nation through your taxes, and the amount of tax you ultimately pay.

Our administration may not believe the wealth is yours or God's. In fact, it acts as though your money belongs to the government to do with as it will! Our current President repeated that concept, in his "You didn't build that" speech – a phrase from one election campaign speech delivered by President Barack Obama on July 13, 2012, in Roanoke, Virginia. The president's remarks included this statement to justify why the government does not believe you "own" your wealth and success: "If you were successful, somebody along the line gave you some help. There was a great teacher somewhere in your life. […] If you've got a business – you didn't build that. Somebody else made that happen." He was heavy on comments that you don't do anything alone, but that lots of people did it for you and with you. But, whatever the case, the government is poised to profit through taxation of your hard-won wealth.[5]

I may be bold, but I would rather quote scripture than any politician:

Genesis 24:35 – *"The Lord has richly blessed my master and he has become very wealthy. The Lord has given him sheep and cattle, silver and gold, male and female servants, and camels and donkeys."*

Always remind yourself that all abundance and wealth is the Lord's – our Lord is the source of our abundance, our opportunities and our successes. Your ability, talent and skill that lead you to your wealth are also God-given, and when you develop those talents you are behaving as a good steward. I take this whole discussion of who creates wealth, and who can dispose of it and how, simply as a reminder to us all that everything we have is from the Lord. We must, in all humility, remember this.

I believe we also take this to mean that in our charity, we must not demand recognition. We need to remain humble. We must not demand our name in lights on a building signboard or on any donor list as thanks for our gift. It is all the Lord's. We are a steward and a manager.

Here is what this also means: *If you yourself do not, consciously and through a personal plan, divert a portion of your wealth to the work of Kingdom, all your self-created assets and those you have stewardship over will be eventually taken by the government for their own purposes and stewardship, in the form of taxation.* Let's put Kingdom first, then Uncle Sam – because we can.

God has allowed you to accumulate and control your wealth, yet governments around the world, including our own, believe they have a better use for it than you. A government will always believe it should be in control of redistributing your wealth for you. Put Kingdom first, then Uncle Sam.

> 2 Chronicles 1:10-12 – "10*[Solomon:] Now give me wisdom and discernment so I can effectively lead this nation. Otherwise, no one is able to make judicial decisions for this great nation of yours."* 11*God said to Solomon, "Because you desire this, and did not ask for riches, wealth, and honor, or for vengeance on your enemies, and because you did not ask for long life, but requested wisdom and discernment so you can make judicial decisions for my people over whom I have made you king,* 12*you are granted wisdom and discernment. Furthermore I am giving you riches, wealth, and honor surpassing that of any king before or after you."*

Another way of looking at this is that Christians don't own anything. We are simply stewards of what God has allowed us to creatively accumulate (with our God-given skill and talent) through His gifts to us and for His purposes. A good steward of God's possessions will not allow the government to tax more than is necessary to fulfill its stated mission. It is little known that one of the explicitly stated purposes of the 1932 estate tax was "redirection of wealth."[6]

Use your new knowledge to direct your wealth in the way the Lord has guided you. Keep in mind your philanthropic goals, the overall context you operate within, and your long-term strategy.

Let us now examine some elements of your potential strategy in the next chapters.

CHAPTER 3

Gifting Insurance

ESTABLISH LIFE INSURANCE POLICIES AS part of your giving strategy. The beneficiaries can be a person, trust, estate, or business. The general rule you are taking advantage of in this strategy is tax reduction. The tax authorities view transferring life insurance policies to a beneficiary as a 'gift' that is subject to the 'gift tax' assessment. However, even though you do not escape taxation entirely, the advantage is clear: the gift tax amount is almost always much less than the corresponding estate tax would have been if the policy remained in your name and your estate. You can pass on more wealth through gifting the policy.

In addition to naming beneficiaries, you can choose to transfer ownership of a life insurance policy; this is generally also done to reduce your estate taxes. If you will be leaving over $5.49M in your estate upon your death (2017 amount), this is a strategy that should interest you. However, once you have transferred the ownership of your policy, keep in mind you no longer have control over it or how it is managed, nor over who the beneficiaries will be.[7]

As one example, you could set up a policy whose beneficiary (or one of them) is your church. Whether you transfer ownership of your policy to your church, or name the church as a beneficiary of the policy you continue to own is a question again of taxation. If you own the policy and die, the entire amount of life insurance funds will be federally taxable in your estate (and thus leave less cash for the beneficiary). Should someone else (i.e. your church) own the policy, the monetary proceeds are not included in your estate; the recipient thus keeps more funds.

Some churches call it "perpetual tithing" when the Church owns (part of) a life-insurance policy on your life; in this case, a portion of your Sunday morning tithes may be applied to pay premiums on the same life insurance policy from which the church benefits. That policy is typically a term life insurance policy.

As another example, you can make your private foundation or Donor Advised Fund (more on these two vehicles below) a beneficiary recipient of the death proceeds of your term life insurance policy or your whole life insurance policy. Only whole life or cash value life insurance has immediate value, whereas a term life insurance policy only has value at the death of insured.

I recommend you tithe or make a free offering of at least 10% of your death benefit proceeds from a life insurance policy to a ministry that has provided you with solace, brotherhood and community, or aid and support of any kind. That ministry becomes one of your named beneficiaries of the policy.

Likewise, you could simply establish a life insurance policy for the *sole* benefit of one ministry, to help fund the Great Commission in this generation, which is summarized in the following verse from The Book of Matthew.

Matthew 28: 18-20 – *[18] Then Jesus came up and said to them, "All authority in heaven and on earth has been given to me. [19] Therefore go and make disciples of all nations, baptizing them in the name of the Father and the Son and the Holy Spirit, [20] teaching them to obey everything I have commanded you. And remember, I am with you always, to the end of the age."*

Many, if not all of you, already own some coverage. Your personal situation may have changed over time since the purchase of that life insurance coverage.

- That policy may no longer be needed for its original intent, such as providing income for a non-working spouse.
- You may have accumulated a substantial estate and no longer need the insurance policy for inheritance purposes.
- The policy type may no longer serve your changed needs.

Be aware that the cash value of a whole life insurance policy can be a useful tool depending on your profession, even though you no longer need the death benefit. The cash value of your life insurance policy, in some cases, can be protected from creditors, lawsuits and even divorce. The cash value of life insurance can even be used for retirement planning purposes.

The mechanics of using insurance policies in charitable giving are fairly straightforward. Leaving the death proceeds of a life insurance policy to a charitable entity can be an inexpensive and highly leveraged giving idea that any person, regardless of resources, can implement. There are five steps to ownership transfer:

1. A donor who wants to make a gift of a life insurance policy must *irrevocably transfer* the ownership of the policy to that charity.

2. The donor must *relinquish* all incidents of ownership and any rights in the policy to the charity, not just the future rights to receive the death benefit. This can be done simply by changing the ownership and beneficiary designation on the policy.
3. The charity or charitable entity will gain *immediate access* to the cash value.
4. You, the donor, continue making premium payments as *gifts* to the entity.
5. You as donor continue to receive immediate *income tax advantages* for an asset that in the alternative would have passed to a charity at death.

NOTE: Be aware that in the gifting of the life insurance policy, the donor does not only give up control, but this strategy may also affect the donor's ability to acquire additional insurance. The face amount of the charity-owned policy still counts against the insured's financial reinsurance limits for underwriting. Inform yourself fully before using this strategy.

Gifts of life insurance policies generally create an income tax deduction equal to the lesser of the policy's fair market value or the donor's cost basis.

EXAMPLE: Assume an insured donor, Cheche, gives a whole life insurance policy with cash value of $100,000 and cumulative premiums of $80,000 to a recognized charity. She does this in a year when her AGI is $140,000. The same year she has already made $10,000 in other charitable contributions. Cheche's income tax deduction for the policy is limited to $80,000 – because it is limited to her basis. Since Cheche's aggregate charitable deductions are limited to $70,000 for the year, she must delay taking the remaining $20,000 until a later year.

CHAPTER 4

Increasing Tax Efficiency

THE HIGHER THE TOP TAX tier, the greater the tax benefits you can reap – when you have a coherent giving strategy.

EXAMPLE: Reducing Overall Tax Rate

- $100,000 charitable gift = tax savings of $35,000 (tax tier of 35%)
- 30% of AGI for non-cash (50% of AGI for cash)

We have a number of ways to give to a charity or a ministry. Individuals can easily make a *gift* outright or use a *trust*, certainly. An individual can also:

- Name a charity as a beneficiary in their *will*
- Designate a charity as beneficiary of their *retirement plan assets*
- Give all or a portion of their *life insurance* to a ministry or registered charity

A charity or ministry is fine, but what is its mission? Align the mission to your own values and passions. Many high net worth households, for instance, value education. They are thus staunch supporters of education in charitable giving. Three-fourths of high net worth households donated to educational organizations from personal assets in 2007, while 21.5% donated to education through their foundations, investment funds, or trusts according to a recent study. You just make sure that the educational organization truly qualifies as such in IRS terms – as is the case for all charitable entities.

CHAPTER 5

Outright Gifts, Giving Cash

1 Corinthians 12:4 – *"Now there are different gifts, but the same Spirit."*

THE MAJORITY OF HIGH NET worth individuals give to charity, yes. Studies have also indicated, alas, that most HNW individuals and families *give inefficiently*! This means their gifts are tax-inefficient for them; often this means that their chosen recipients receive less, too.

In this country, the majority of our wealth is in *non-cash assets*. We have said it: We can give gifts of our cash wealth <u>and</u> gifts of non-cash property and other non-cash assets.

You can always make outright gifts of cash to your favorite charity or your church, certainly. Outright cash gifts are so welcomed! They are the type of gift that benefits the charity, church or synagogue immediately, even exclusively.

"Outright gifts" are defined as gifts (not only cash) with no strings attached for the recipients. If your outright gift is to a registered charity/non-profit, you receive an immediate income tax charitable deduction or a gift tax deduction from your taxes that year. According to IRS publication 526, you can make deductible contributions of *money or property* to churches, synagogues, temples, and other registered religious organizations.

OTHER GIVING
Citizens can give to federal, state, and local governments! The conditions? The contribution must be solely for public purposes (for example, a gift to reduce the public debt, a gift to maintain a specific public park).

You can make deductible contributions to schools and hospitals, as well as to support organizations like Boy Scouts of America, Girl Scouts of America, Boys and Girls Clubs of America, and war veterans' support groups. Just make sure they are registered non-profit entities as outlined by the IRS.

The out-of-pocket expenses you incur are deductible when you volunteer in a qualified social welfare organization such as The Salvation Army, American Red Cross, CARE, Goodwill Industries, United Way or C.A.S.T. The expenses are all deductible as charitable contributions to that non-profit. You can even deduct expenses you paid for a student living with you, if that student is sponsored by a qualified organization.

NOT DEDUCTIBLE
Contributions that are *not deductible as charitable* include:

- Money or property that you give to civic leagues, social or sports clubs, labor unions, or chambers of commerce
- Most giving to foreign organizations (*except certain "qualified" charities – see below*)
- Groups that are run for personal profit

- Groups whose purpose is to lobby for law changes, homeowners' associations, individual political groups or candidates for public office
- Money paid to raffles, bingo, or for lottery tickets
- Dues, fees, or bills paid to country clubs, lodges, fraternal orders, or similar groups
- Tuition
- Value of your time or services
- Value of blood given to a blood bank

QUALIFIED ORGANIZATIONS

Not all charitable contributions are tax deductible. As stated above, not all of your desired charitable contributions will qualify to be tax deductions. Primarily of interest are the foreign charities here (most of which are not eligible), but it is good to know how the IRS categorizes eligibility for tax deduction purposes.

The entities must be "qualified organizations" according to the IRS code. Internal Revenue Service (IRS) Publication 78 states that qualified organizations are charities, non-profit organizations and religious organizations that are "organized or created in the United States or its possessions, or under the laws of the United States, any State, the District of Columbia or any possession of the United States, and organized and operated exclusively for charitable, religious, educational, scientific, or literary purposes, or for the prevention of cruelty to children or animals." Thus, if your preferred charity is not registered in the US, it is not likely that the IRS will allow you to get a charitable tax deduction. You can go ahead with the gift; just don't expect a tax deduction.

The bottom line is to make certain that the charity is a qualified charity under the IRS code. Get a written receipt, if possible, or keep a good bank record of any cash donations.

Also, get a written receipt for any non-cash donation. More on non-cash giving now.

CHAPTER 6

Asset-Based Giving

Acts 2:45 – "…and they began selling their property and possessions and distributing the proceeds to everyone, as anyone had need."

ANOTHER STRATEGY FOR MORE EFFICIENT giving is to bequeath highly appreciated *non-cash* assets in your portfolio. Too many individuals think about their wealth for charitable giving purposes only in terms of their cash accounts. This, however, is faulty thinking! 80% of all charitable giving may come from our collective cash reserves – but most of our wealth (90%, say some estimates) is actually in non-cash assets. And this type of non-cash asset can easily be bequeathed to charity! There are many benefits to doing so, both for you and for the charitable organization.

An IRS statistic indeed shows that most people give from cash resources, even though the bulk of American wealth is held in non-cash assets. This non-cash wealth can include:

- Business ownership, whether LLC, S or C Corp or shares in a limited or general partnership
- Real estate holdings
- Retirement fund assets
- Marketable securities – stocks, mutual funds, bonds, etc. in your portfolio

- Closely-held company stock
- Oil or gas interests; mining interests
- Agricultural assets – farmland or forestry ownership, other land
- Insurance assets

The best assets to give are the ones that maximize your charitable giving potential, but also minimize your taxes and the taxes anyone else may owe on that asset. Look beneath the tip of the iceberg for this type of wealth that you have in your possession. Donating 5%, 10% – or an even greater portion of any of this type of non-cash asset – represents real advantages to you. By donating non-cash assets such as stock, real estate, or a business interest before any sale, you can firstly reduce your own taxes, and secondly send more to the Kingdom than you ever dreamed possible.

By donating non-cash U.S. assets first – rather than selling them first, paying taxes, and donating the net proceeds – givers will typically receive a *tax deduction* for the full fair-market value of the gift, as well as *avoid capital gains taxes*. The capital gains taxes they save by giving the asset directly to a church, charity or a charity advised fund means more goes to support the work of God's Kingdom.

EXAMPLE: One new type of retirement fund asset was created by Congress on January 1, 2013, with the new American Taxpayer Relief Act of 2012 (ATRA). An important provision of ATRA covers the *IRA Charitable Rollover*. This allows an IRA owner to transfer up to $100,000 per year to a qualified charity from his IRA assets. IRA charitable rollovers are tax-free and amounts in the account not included in your adjusted gross income (AGI).

The majority of my clients never use or need the assets in their IRA. As a result, they simply end up paying taxes on the required minimum distribution (RMD). Consequently, a non-spouse heir ends up paying ordinary taxes on the distribution even before reaching age 70½. Instead of paying taxes on the required minimum distribution, a non-spouse beneficiary should consider making this type of charitable rollover. *IRA charitable rollovers qualify as the donor's RMD.*

Givers will receive the full tax deduction for the fair market value for donations of non-cash assets such as:

- Appreciated securities – stocks, bonds, and mutual funds
- Real estate – land, houses, farms, commercial properties and so on

You will see greater savings on your personal income tax returns by gifting non-cash assets, as you know. By paying less in taxes, more money will stay in your pocket for your own lifestyle expenses – and for additional giving to the Kingdom and the Lord's purpose that is communicated to you.

Despite the fact that 90% of all wealth is held in non-cash assets, 80% of giving is still done in cash, and only 20% of giving is done in non-cash assets. Look at your non-cash assets; do your giving differently and more effectively from now on.

This is worth repeating. Your non-cash assets may be the most beneficial type asset to give to charity because:

1. It is more tax efficient for you: No capital gains taxes. That savings can be significant!

2. More to give: No capital gains tax means money remains in your pocket. You will have more to contribute in support of the work of God's Kingdom.
3. Fair Market Value is your calculation: Individuals receive a tax deduction for the full fair market value of the gift.

CHAPTER 7

Beneficiary Designation

Matthew 19:29 – *"And whoever has left houses or brothers or sisters or father or mother or children or fields for My sake will receive a hundred times as much and will inherit eternal life."*

AN INDIVIDUAL CAN GIVE GIFTS by including a provision in a will or trust document or by using a beneficiary designation form from a bank or other financial institution. The charity will receive the gift at your death, when you go home to be with the Lord and ultimately hear, "Well done, good and faithful steward," and at which time your estate can take the income and estate tax deduction from the property you left to charity.

Although the discussion in this book is on transferring assets while you are alive, the Transfer on Death (TOD) form can be obtained from your own bank or other financial institution. The TOD registrations allow you to pass the securities or cash in your own accounts directly to another person or entity (your "TOD beneficiary") upon your death without having to go through probate. By setting up your account or having your securities registered this way, the executor or administrator of your estate will not have to take any additional action to ensure that your securities transfer to whomever you have designated. However, TOD *beneficiaries* must take steps to re-register the securities in their names after the death of the account owner. This typically involves sending a copy of the death certificate and an application for re-registration to a transfer agent.

Many types of vehicles are available to individual donors for charitable giving, with Foundations and Donor Advised Funds being two of the most popular. We will look at these vehicles in the next two chapters. Although they are structured and operate differently from each other, they both offer tax deductions, with the stipulation that the donated funds are used to make future grants to recognized charities.

CHAPTER 8

Private Non-Operating Foundation

A PRIVATE FOUNDATION IS A freestanding corporate entity that applies for and receives its own tax-exempt status. It thus has greater freedoms but also heavier responsibilities and requirements for its operations than the Donor Advised Fund (which I discuss next). There is much potential for greater control by the donor with private foundations.

All 501(c)(3) charities are classified by the IRS as either a private foundation or as a public charity. A private foundation receives its funding from one or few donors (who can be an individual, an entire family or a business entity), rather than from a broader, more anonymous, general public.

A *private operating foundation* distributes funds to its own programs that exist for recognized charitable purposes. A *private non-operating foundation* grants money to other charitable organizations and their programs; it is not operating any programs of its own.

Perhaps the only reasons to have a private foundation are to give to someone individually, or to hire a family member to run the foundation and pay her a salary. If you have this interest, you will need to focus on the private (non-operating) foundation, which is the most commonly used vehicle for family giving. A private (non-operating) foundation may receive its proceeds from an endowment or bequest if it is a "pass-through" foundation and from periodic gifts of assets.

Very often, a single "high capacity" or wealthy family will form such a private foundation as a charity that invests dollars and uses those dollars to make financial grants to other charities. A private foundation generally supports charitable programs directly, providing grants to other nonprofit organizations rather than operating programs of its own.

Churches, schools, hospitals, medical research organizations and some governmental units are the "traditional" public charities. If the private foundation decides to give a scholarship and grants that scholarship to an individual, that private foundation must gain IRS approval. The scholarship and grants must be pursuant to a program approved in advance by the IRS and the decision to give money must be made on an objective and non-discriminatory basis.

Private foundations generally are a good fit for families who want to maximize control over their gifted assets. But they must be willing to invest the additional time and money that it takes to manage the more complex administrative and legal requirements for a private foundation. There are huge numbers of complex government regulations, constraints on types of activities, taxes and large expenses (not least of which is qualified administrative personnel) as well as numerous unique limitations associated with a private foundation.

Do you still want to establish that private foundation with all its fees, paperwork and headaches? A starting point of $1 Million or $2 Million may not be a sufficient enough amount to establish a private foundation unless you only desire bragging rights at the local country club. Your personal CPA and your attorney will be two happy individuals that you established that private foundation, because you would have contributed to their kids' orthodontics or college tuition. The fees can be that onerous! Even if you can contribute several million, there is a more efficient lower cost alternative to the private foundation. We explore it in the next chapter.

CHAPTER 9

Donor Advised Fund

1 Chronicles 29:16 – *"O Lord our God, all this wealth, which we have collected to build a temple for you to honor your holy name, comes from you; it all belongs to you."*

A GIVING VEHICLE THAT IS becoming more popular is the Donor Advised Fund (DAF).

A Donor Advised Fund is a charitable giving vehicle held within and managed or administered by a public charity, which itself was created to manage charitable donations on behalf of organizations, families, or individuals.

We find these types of sponsoring organizations offering Donor Advised Funds to donors today:

- National sponsoring organizations
- Community foundations
- Public foundations
- Other public charities like universities or hospitals (that primarily support their own programs or goals)

If it sounds confusing, it is more complex than your average investment vehicle. Simply stated, the Donor Advised Fund provides a way for you as one individual or family to manage your overall giving from one source. In spite of appearances, it is easy to set up, low-cost, and flexible when you are making gifts to multiple organizations.

You, the donor, open an account in the fund and deposit cash or other financial instruments (see below) – which the Donor Advised Fund administers to make your gifts. You give up ownership of the deposited assets but have input on how and where gifts are made.

Donor Advised Funds work well for people who are already giving. It can reduce administrative nightmares by having one place or one organization to administer all of your charitable giving desires. You don't have to keep writing checks, keeping receipts for all of these different ministries or non-profits that you support. It is great tool for families that already have a private foundation.

DONOR ADVISED FUND VS. PRIVATE FOUNDATION

	Donor Advised Funds	Private Foundations
Control of grants and assets	Donor may recomend grants and investments, but the sponsoring charity makes all final decisions	Donor family has a complete control of all grantmaking and investment decisions, subject to self-dealing rules
Required Grant Distribution	None	Must expend 5% of net assets value annually, regardless of how much the assets earn
Privacy	Names of individual donors can be kept confidential if desired	Must file detailed and public tax returns on grants, investment fees, trustee fees, staff salaries, etc
Administrative Responsibilities	Recommend grants to favorite charitable causes	Manage assets, keep records, select charities, administer grants, file state and federal tax returns, maintain board minutes, etc.
Governance & Succession	Donor(s) may name advisors to recommend grants and investments; Donors may also name successors to the account, and ensure a continuing legacy	Opportunities for board selection, training and bringing in the next generation are greater; No restrictions regarding who serves on the board
Perpetuity	Can exist in perpetuity	Can exist in perpetuity

Families who have established a Donor Advised Fund can continue giving to multiple charities even after the original donor has left this world, by naming children as successor trustees. A Donor Advised Fund can receive those non-cash assets that I have been encouraging you to bequeath more liberally, i.e., appreciated securities such as stocks, bonds, and mutual funds, real estate and houses, other properties and interest in businesses. When a donor gifts assets to the Donor Advised Fund, the donor receives an immediate tax deduction according to IRS guidelines.

An individual can avoid or minimize capital gains taxes by establishing a Donor Advised Fund and then transferring assets to the Donor Advised Fund, subsequently minimizing the size of an estate in order to avoid estate or gift taxes (See Appendix A case study).

A giver can use a Donor Advised Fund to gain greater control over the use of donations.

If you give to a large organization with many different areas the organization supports, say the United Way or American Cancer Society, you will not have any way of influencing specific areas that the particular charity is serving. Establish your own Donor Advised Fund. With a Donor Advised Fund that you advise, you can then recommend that certain funds are made available to a specific charity or end user, instead of giving the money to a charity that can disburse the funds however its leaders see fit.

Only the income generated by the Donor Advised Fund needs to be distributed. There are also a few money management firms like Nepsis Capital Management and Stewardship

Partners that can manage Socially Responsible Investing (SRI) or even Biblically Responsible Investments (BRI), if that is what you desire as donor.

Today, contributions to Donor Advised Funds are almost $7.5 billion annually, and the average account size has increased to more than $226,000 (so you see that it does not take the many millions that a private foundation might to get started). Popularity is also due to:

- Donor Advised Funds can recommend specific end users and have more control over where the money ends up.
- For a giver who desires to leave a substantial charitable legacy, the giver could name a Donor Advised Fund to receive the death benefits of a life insurance policy.
- The Donor Advised Fund is ideal for givers who have beliefs that make the privacy of giving a vital factor, regardless of amounts/types/destinations of their donations.
- A donor can maintain privacy of giving with a Donor Advised Fund – doing their giving anonymously as opposed to through a private foundation or a public charity where the giving must be declared.

CHAPTER 10

Structuring Charitable Giving Vehicles

LET'S LOOK AS AN EXAMPLE at the structure and operations of a Donor Advised Fund. Since most of these funds can be created, set up and administered primarily online, overhead administrative costs incurred by the sponsoring organization usually are very minimal.

SET UP AND FUNDING

Most individuals who desire to establish a formal giving program will start with an asset that they want to give away. This type of asset is made to order as a gift to the Donor Advised Fund (since one gives up the asset entirely and the Donor Advised Fund is a separate entity from the donor). The asset is typically cash, but please recall that it can be non-cash, such as highly appreciated securities, a percentage business interest or any illiquid hard-to-value assets.

Donors who own or control a business can channel business income from the business entity directly to charity. You can transfer business property or a business interest directly to the Donor Advised Fund for greater control and flexibility of charitable assets. Typically, as stated elsewhere, it's a transfer of less than 10% of the value of the business, so there is no real loss of control of the business entity.

In many cases, it does not require a large gift to get started. A Donor Advised Fund can be established with initial donations of just $10,000, and some organizations will allow you to establish a Donor Advised Fund for a much smaller amount. Sponsoring organizations will allow you to choose a third party money manager for as little as $50,000. Remember, choosing a skilled third-party money manager will allow you to give from the income that the funds are able to generate, rather than from the principal.

Your gift is now the property of the Donor Advised Fund. You, the donor, now have advisory status with the Donor Advised Fund. You are now the advisor to the fund and can give recommendations to the sponsoring organization administering the Fund. The sponsoring organization is not legally bound to you. The sponsoring organization makes gifts to other public charities on your recommendations. The sponsoring organization will perform the due diligence for you to make certain that the grantee has tax-exempt status.

The individuals or families who use a Donor Advised Fund are donors who have a charitable intent and are looking for an efficient way to give. Giving at this level can begin with a donor who wants to be obedient to:

1 Timothy 6:17-18 – *"[17] Command those who are rich in this world's goods not to be haughty or to set their hope on riches, which are uncertain, but on God who richly provides us with all things for our enjoyment. [18] Tell them to do good, to be rich in good deeds, to be generous givers, sharing with others."*

A donor can name the Donor Advised Fund whatever they want, with or without using the family's name. For example, my family's Donor Advised Fund is named the Stephenson Orafu Foundation.

The Donor Advised Fund will receive the funds, and the sponsoring organization or third party administrator (such as Waterstone or the National Christian Foundation/NCF) will

- Hold the funds
- Invest the funds within Donor Advised Fund -held investment accounts
- Liquidate the assets (i.e., real property) when it is time for gifting them
- Process any distribution request to gift funds to any approved 501(c)(3) organization
- Provide centralized administration, record-keeping and filing obligations – no matter how many organizations you put on your giving list – including providing tax deduction documentation for you

All you have to do is to identify the charitable recipients and the DAF administrators or sponsoring organization will help you identify the most tax efficient way to give.

Management

It's very important, as I mentioned earlier, that you find a qualified financial advisor with a clear Kingdom philosophy and strategy for managing money.

Once your gifts have been assigned to the DAF, you have as much time as you need to decide how to disperse the funds to the ultimate recipient or recipients. The advisor assists you as to how assets in the DAF will be managed (invested, primarily, until donation). It is important for you to know that the assets in the DAF are earning an acceptable rate of return.

The donor decides what assets are going to be contributed to the DAF and simply makes a recommendation on what charitable recipients the DAF will service. Charitable recipients could be

- Your own or other local churches or spiritual organizations
- Non-profit groups whose objective corresponds to your passions, beliefs and values, that engage God while serving others – educational, research, social types of non-profits, etc.
- Rotary, Lions or other service clubs you belong to or believe in – as long as they have their own federally recognized charitable organization or 501(c)(3) determination allowing you to make a tax-*deductible* gift**
- A local community foundation

**A gift to a Rotary, Lion's or Kiwanis Club is not generally tax-deductible, so check whether the club is registered.

Since a donor simply advises or makes recommendations to the sponsoring organization, the donor can say to the sponsoring organization "disburse $20,000 to this charity" or "disperse $5,000 for that charity." It is important to remember that a donor simply makes a recommendation to the fund as mentioned earlier. Gifts or charitable grants to a recipient can be made anonymously to provide for confidentiality. A donor may feel it is important that the recipient not know where the gift came from. (Remember, there is no public filing requirements as there are with private foundations, so it is impossible for the charity to identify where the gift came from if there is a desire by the donor to remain anonymous.)

A donor can have the money invested in an investment account within the Donor Advised Fund so you can give away the *original principal as well as the growth.* By utilizing a clear investment strategy and philosophy with a skilled money manager, it's possible to give away a lot more than you had originally gifted, all the while avoiding paying capital gains taxes. A donor could possibly give away twice as much money as originally gifted to the Donor Advised Fund, since the actual dollars can be invested with a professional money manager, as mentioned earlier.

EXAMPLE: Stewardship Partners (www.stewardshippartners.com) is highly focused on Biblically Responsible Investing (BRI), if that is a choice you wish to make.

Philanthropic Children

A Donor Advised Fund is the ideal charitable vehicle for training the next generation of family members in generosity, planned giving and strategic thinking, and getting them involved in charitable decision-making during your own lifetime so that they can honorably carry it on after your death.

In "Raising Philanthropic Children," from an Indiana University (IU)/Bank of America (BAC) survey, setting an example for children or other young people was an important motivator for about half of the donors surveyed who decided to establish a giving vehicle. More and more parents are actually involving their younger and adult-age children in decisions about grant-making and the charitable organizations they choose to support. In fact, over 95% of high net worth households instruct their children about philanthropy and the value of giving. More than 60% of wealthy donors actively involve their children in philanthropy according to the IU/BAC study.

Demonstrating the effectiveness of their parents' teaching, nearly 40% of the adult-age children of wealthy families say they now give through their own private foundation or Donor Advised Fund because of the example and education provided by their parents.

Grant requests from the DAF can be met either during the donor's lifetime or by the donor's testamentary instructions with the DAF in the event of death. A donor can have instructions that state, "If I still have money in the fund on the date of my death, I want those funds disbursed in the following way." The donor appoints grant makers such as their children so that upon death, they can assign the charities that will receive the remainder of the assets. Donors may desire to create or leave a charitable legacy during their lifetime that continues after death.

DONOR ADVISED FUND OR PRIVATE FOUNDATION?
Without going into any more detail about the differences between a Donor Advised Fund and a (perhaps more familiar) private non-operating foundation, I include the following chart to summarize the main distinctions between the two.

DONOR ADVISED FUND VS. PRIVATE FOUNDATION

	Donor Advised Funds	Private Foundations
Start Up Time	Immediate	Can take several weeks or months
Start Up	Typically none (often covered by sponsoring charity); Can be established immediately	Legal Fees and other start up costs can be substantial; Typically takes several weeks, and often a few months to create
Costs Ongoing Administrative and Management Fees	Varies with sponsoring charity and level of services; typicaly less than supporting organizations or private foundations	Varies with choice of board, and level of services required; Must file annual tax returns, conduct independent audit, manage and administer all functions
Tax deduction limits for gifts of cash	50% of adjusted gross income	30% of adjusted gross income
Tax deduction limits for gifts of stock or real property	30% of adjusted gross income	20% of adjusted gross income
Excise Taxes	None	Excise tax of 1% to 2% of net investment income annually
Valuation of gifts	Fair market value	Fair market value for cash and publicly traded stock; Cost basis for gifts of closely held stock or real property

CHAPTER 11

A Charitable Remainder Trust

WE ALL KNOW THIS CHAPTER of the New Testament that we have come to call The Way of Love:

> 1 Corinthians 13 – *"If I speak in the tongues of men and of angels, but I do not have love, I am a noisy gong or a clanging cymbal. And if I have prophecy, and know all mysteries and all knowledge, and if I have all faith so that I can remove mountains, but do not have love, I am nothing. If I give away everything I own, and if I give over my body in order to boast, but do not have love, I receive no benefit. [...]"*

> Acts 10:3-4 – *"About three o'clock one afternoon he saw clearly in a vision an angel of God who came in and said to him, 'Cornelius.' Staring at him and becoming greatly afraid, Cornelius replied, 'What is it, Lord?' The angel said to him, 'Your prayers and your acts of charity have gone up as a memorial before God.'"*

BRING IT ALL TOGETHER

The tool of choice for my estate planning clients who desire to both leave a legacy for the next generation and a substantial gift to charity has been the Charitable Remainder Trust (CRT).

CRTs come in three types:

1. Charitable Remainder Annuity Trust (CRAT), which pays a fixed dollar amount, usually annually
2. Charitable Remainder Unitrust (CRUT), which pays a fixed percentage of the trust's value annually
3. Charitable Pooled Income Fund, which is set up by a charity enabling many donors to contribute to the fund

Your primary purpose in creating a charitable remainder trust is to reduce taxes – this is an admirable personal goal, but I repeat that it fills a Kingdom role as well. It leaves *much more wealth* available for your beneficiary. You do this with a CRT by donating assets into the trust and then having it pay your designated beneficiary for a stated period of time. Once this deadline has expired, the rest of the assets in the trust – the "remainder" – is transferred to the charities you also named as your CRT beneficiaries.

If it is time to incorporate giving into your overall estate and financial planning design, this may be the perfect opportunity to incorporate a CRT into your giving strategy. It is particularly for givers with highly appreciated assets who are looking to reduce their estate while still providing for their loved ones. You must consider the CRT along with your primary tool, the Donor Advised Fund for charitable giving, simply for the financial benefits that these tools create for you, the Kingdom and your loved ones.

Philosophy

A CRT can make the most of a highly appreciated asset by minimizing both income and estate taxes. It can be a smart alternative to selling an asset and incurring capital gains tax, as discussed in earlier chapters. A giver can simply include the asset in the trust to provide for one or more surviving loved ones, or outright give the asset to charity or their charitable giving vehicle.

A CRT can help givers avoid capital gains tax, utilize an immediate income tax deduction, increase their income, and ultimately provide for their favorite charities through a charitable giving vehicle such as a Donor Advised Fund.

SET UP AND FUNDING

Please be aware that a CRT is not just any type of trust! With the CRT, a grantor places certain assets into a trust, the remainder of which will eventually pass to one or more charitable beneficiaries known as "remainder beneficiaries", which can be your DAF or private foundation. Before the assets pass to the charity, however, they produce income that passes to certain non-charitable beneficiaries known as income beneficiaries – you. The grantor names both the charitable and the income beneficiaries.

The CRT arrangement simply involves the transfer of certain assets into a trust for the present benefit of a non-charitable or income beneficiary, with the terms of the trust requiring that the remainder be a gift to a charity or a charitable giving vehicle such as a Donor Advised Fund or private non-operating foundation.

NOTE: In order to qualify as a CRT, the *remainder beneficiary* must always be a qualified charitable organization. To be a qualified charity, the organization or institution must be organized and operated exclusively for one or more of the purposes set forth in Section 501(c)(3) of the Internal Revenue Code, while none of its earnings may come to any private shareholder or individual.

Generally, the grantor will fund a CRT with highly appreciated assets on which the grantor would owe significant capital gains taxes were they to be sold outright. In lieu of paying capital gains taxes, the grantor is entitled to a tax deduction that is partly based on the appreciated value of the assets placed into a CRT, up to the limits permitted by IRS rules, in the year in which the grantor *establishes the CRT.* The grantor may be the income beneficiary or the trustee.

IRREVOCABILITY: AN ESSENTIAL DISTINCTION

It is important to note that CRTs are *always irrevocable* – meaning that once the arrangement is made, *it may not be changed.*

This said, the named charitable beneficiaries may be changed to another charity under certain circumstances. If you have named the charitable beneficiary to be a Donor Advised Fund or private foundation, this becomes a moot point. If you name your own charitable giving vehicle as the charitable beneficiary, then you can give to multiple charities and you do not have to concern yourself about any one named charitable beneficiary.

If a trust is established so that a charity receives the remainder, but it is a *revocable* trust, it does not qualify as a CRT, and thus does not receive the same favorable tax treatment to which CRTs are entitled.

MANAGEMENT

A Charitable Remainder Trust achieves asset protection (a shield from creditors), while still using the same protected assets to produce income for you during your lifetime. All you have to do to reap these benefits, so to speak, is irrevocably assign those same assets to the CRT! It may sound extreme, but is highly advantageous. Retaining control is one such advantage.

The grantor is the individual who establishes the trust and makes all the important decisions involved in doing so. The grantor owns the assets, also known as the "corpus" or the "principal," that are placed in the trust. The grantor names the trustee, designates beneficiaries, and defines the terms of the trust to be set forth in the trust document.

Therefore, through the instructions dictated by the grantor in the trust document, the grantor makes one of the most important decisions in the entire CRT process, which is *how the trust assets will be managed and distributed*. That represents personal control.

A grantor/giver can still direct money towards the charity of his choice, especially a giving vehicle the grantor advises, instead of handing it over to the government in the form of taxes. If the grantor so desires, a Wealth Replacement Trust (more in the next chapter) funded by life insurance can be established to replace the trust assets to ensure that the grantor's heirs are provided for as well. More control.

While the tax advantages of CRTs make them valuable estate and financial planning tools, you need to make certain that your financial planner, tax advisor and attorney are all in accord with a Kingdom approach when it comes the establishment and the dispositions of your CRT.

Beneficiaries: Individuals and Charities

The *trust* beneficiaries are the parties chosen by the grantor that receive the benefits of the trust assets. The *income* beneficiaries are those who receive income from the trust and who receive payments for their lifetime or for a specified period.

In a CRT, the income beneficiary is usually an individual, or some entity that is not classified as a charitable organization. Income beneficiaries may be any living person or existing entity chosen by the grantor, including the grantor's children, ex-spouses, or relatives with special needs. The grantor is most often the income beneficiary in the case of a CRT.

The income stream may be paid to the beneficiaries for a stated period, so long as the period is measured by the life expectancy of an existing person also known as a "life in being", or a finite term not to exceed 20 years. The amount of income that may be paid out depends upon the value of the trust assets and the type of CRT created by the grantor, such as a Charitable Remainder Annuity Trust (CRAT), or a Charitable Remainder Unitrust (CRUT). These are variations on the basic CRT; they allow for even greater flexibility. Your advisor can discuss the differences with you.

Just like the income beneficiaries, the charitable beneficiaries are chosen by the grantor. The remainder beneficiaries are entitled to receive the balance of the trust property *after the income beneficiaries are no longer entitled to any income payment*. This will often be the last step in the process. I recommend that you should consider making your Donor Advised Fund the remainder beneficiary of any CRT assets.

CHAPTER 12

Wealth Replacement Trust with a CRT

> 1 Chronicles 29:28 – *"He died at a good old age, having enjoyed long life, wealth, and honor."*

IF THE GRANTOR HAS CHOSEN to establish a Wealth Replacement Trust, then there is another step to making the CRT process complete.

Placing assets in a CRT unquestionably removes them from the grantor's estate, and many givers fear that the remaining property in their estate may be insufficient to provide for both the charity and their loved ones.

However, givers do not have to choose between the two. Through an Irrevocable Life Insurance Trust or a Wealth Replacement Trust, whole life insurance may be used to replace the wealth that, if not for the charitable contribution, would have been left to heirs.

SET UP AND FUNDING

The grantor establishes an irrevocable trust to purchase a whole life insurance policy. The goal is to replace the CRT assets that would otherwise be left to the heirs with life insurance proceeds. The goal is to replace the entire value of the asset, or at least cover the value of the remainder interest, so a whole life policy can be chosen to meet this need.

Although the trust will require that premiums be paid to maintain the protection of the policy, the CRT provides the funds for those payments. The Wealth Replacement Trust will be funded with distributions from the CRT. The income earned by the CRT will be earmarked to pay premiums of the policy held in the Wealth Replacement Trust. The tax savings obtained from the charitable income tax deduction will offset the insurance premiums.

Buying a whole life insurance policy can be a less expensive way to replace the value of the donated assets. Premium dollars can be leveraged to provide thousands of dollars' worth of life insurance protection, especially if the CRT income is directed towards the payment of premiums. Furthermore, by using an irrevocable trust to purchase the whole life insurance policy, the whole life insurance and its proceeds are outside the probate estate of the insured and will pass to the giver's beneficiaries free of federal income and estate taxes.

Remember that the Wealth Replacement Trust is an *optional* step of the CRT process and is only utilized when a grantor wants to leave a charitable legacy and still provide for heirs and loved ones. Like any other trust, a Wealth Replacement Trust should only be established with the guidance of a qualified financial advisor, tax advisor and attorney to be sure that it will not trigger any federal gift tax liability.

Subsequently, if the grantor chooses to fund a life insurance policy within an Irrevocable Life Insurance Trust, the last step of the CRT process occurs upon the death of the insured, when a payment is made to the trust. This payment is made free of federal income and estate tax; the trustee distributes the proceeds to the beneficiaries based on the trust agreement. From the heirs' perspective, this may be the most important step because it provides them with an increased inheritance that passes to them, free of estate and income tax, upon the death of the last income beneficiary. The benefits of CRTs, as we have seen, are as follows:

- The grantor benefits because a tax deduction will be available for the charitable contribution.
- Capital gains taxes on appreciated property can be avoided or deferred.
- The giver may receive either an income payment or conveniently provide for a loved one with those payments.
- The heirs chiefly benefit from wealth replacement planning because they receive the proceeds free of estate and income tax, and will receive them without having to go through the probate process. More wealth; less time spent securing it.
- When a Wealth Replacement Trust is established, the assets placed in the trust will be replaced with life insurance for the beneficiary.
- The charitable entity benefits because that entity will be receiving a charitable donation.

A CRT can be a positive endeavor for all parties involved. A prudent financial advisor will evaluate all relevant information to ensure that this is an investment that's right for you and your family.

CHAPTER 13

What Strategy is the Best Strategy?

> Acts 10:2 – *"He was a devout, God-fearing man, as was all his household; he did many acts of charity for the people and prayed to God regularly."*

IF YOU ARE CONTEMPLATING A Kingdom giving strategy, you first need a clear and accurate picture of the Lord's purpose for your wealth. The answers are very personal and come from prayer and quiet communion with God. I find that this step makes all subsequent mechanics, decision-making and actions very easy!

Next, your need a clear accounting of your assets and your income – and the valuation of those assets. Also keep in mind your age, who your beneficiaries are to be and why, your long-term goals as well as your shorter-term cash needs, and other criteria that a qualified advisor can help you determine if you need that assistance.

The following questions will help identify which charitable giving vehicle might be most suitable for you.

- Do you wish to use the fund to hire staff in order to pursue a charitable mission (that is, design and operate programs of some kind)?
- Do you wish to make grants to individuals, such as for hardship?
- Do you wish to make grants to charitable projects being carried out by existing for-profit organizations?
- Do you want control over investment management?
- Do you want final say over grant making decisions?
- Are you willing to meet a 5% minimum annual charitable distribution requirement?

If the answer to one or more of the above questions is an unequivocal "Yes," it is likely that you the giver will benefit from allocating at least a portion of your dollars to a private foundation.

The Donor Advised Fund, of course, does remain a great solution to consider instead of, or in addition to, a private foundation. Answering some additional questions about a DAF helps clarify the circumstances and priorities for you as the giver:

- Does the difference in tax deduction limits against the AGI make a difference to you?
- Is the reduction of initial setup costs a high priority?
- Are you prepared to select a board, operate a grant making program, and manage an organization or even hire someone to handle all the responsibilities on its behalf?
- Do you wish to remain anonymous with some or all grants?
- Do you wish to highlight issue areas or legacies with name acknowledgment?

- Do you want the responsibility of ensuring that grantees or their projects are legally approved?
- Do you already have access to expertise with valuing and documenting any planned donations of non-cash or non-publicly traded assets?

DEDUCTION ORDER

The deduction order for most donors – income tax deductions for charitable contributions by individuals – is straightforward. For donors who give only to a Donor Advised Fund or a public charity, the rules are reasonably direct. Cash gifts are deducted first. Appreciated gifts are deducted next. If there is an available 50% or 30% limit, then carry-forwards of cash and appreciated property are deducted in order, with the oldest carry-forward gifts deducted first.

The deduction order could also be fairly sophisticated. The deduction order as a percent of contribution base could be as follows:

- Cash gifts to 50% AGI limit
- Appreciated gifts elected to be deducted at cost basis to 50% limit
- Unrelated use tangible personal property deducted at cost basis to 50% limit
- Short-term capital gain deducted at cost basis to 50% limit
- Appreciated stock or land deducted at fair market value to 30% limit
- Gifts "for the use of" a charity deducted to 30% limit
- Cash to private foundation deducted at 30% limit

- Public stock to private foundation deducted at fair market value to 20% limit
- Land or private stock to private foundation at cost basis to 20% limit
- Carry-forwards of 50% limit gifts
- Carry-forwards of 30% limit cash gifts to private foundations
- Carry-forwards of 30% appreciated property gifts to public foundations
- Carry-forwards of 20% limit gifts to private foundations

CHAPTER 14

Conclusion

2 Corinthians 9:7 – *"Each one of you should give just as he has decided in his heart, not reluctantly or under compulsion, because God loves a cheerful giver."*

EACH ONE OF YOU SHOULD give just as you have decided in your heart, not reluctantly or under out of any sense of family or social pressures. God – and all recipients of your generosity – loves a cheerful giver!

I obviously did not write this for people who are trying to get rich, but for those who are already rich by this world's standards. The book was written for those who want to experience personal satisfaction and fulfillment in life by giving efficiently to charity.

When the apostle Paul said, Philippians 4:17 – *"I do not say this because I am seeking a gift. Rather, I seek the credit that abounds to your account."*

Paul is simply explaining how God wants faithful men and women to act as conduits for getting His wealth around the world – not simply for personal gain, but for Kingdom purposes.

In Andy Stanley's book, *'Fields of Gold'*, he remarks, "God is up to something in this world when we get involved with Him in this way (the way of generous giving)."

The question that I have asked you to answer for yourself is,

"Would you be open to paying zero estate tax to the government by giving it to charity instead, if it would not materially impact the amount you leave your children?"

and

"Do you want to receive a charitable deduction for this year?"

This book gives you as donor a number of ideas to enable you to create a formal strategic plan for giving that is both right with man (the IRS and our worldly laws) and pleasing to God (his design for our lifetime).

You can now begin to bless organizations that have had (or are still creating) a beneficial influence on you. Now you are in a position to benefit others even more than before, with the tools and strategies you have developed by reading this book.

Morgan Stanley advertisement from 2006:

"You must pay taxes. But there's no law that says you gotta leave a tip."

I'm not asking you to do anything unreasonable – it's very simple. You can place your wealth in a vehicle giving tremendous benefit to the Kingdom ... or you can allow the government to take it in the form of high taxes imposed on you, the wealthy individual and wealthy business owner. Render to Caesar, so to speak, or render to God. You do have the choice!

Remember, the IRS allows all U.S. taxpayers to deduct up to 50% of adjusted gross income (AGI) each year as a charitable contribution deduction. The majority of U.S. taxpayers never reach their giving potential. Far too many individuals are incapable of even defining their giving potential!

In my financial and advisory practice, I try to give fellow Christians the tools and techniques necessary to increase their giving to charity. Every year, my clients ask me, "How can I reduce the amount of income taxes that I must pay to the IRS?" After reviewing their income tax return from the previous year, I frequently notice that they either have not given or have given very little to charity.

I typically then explain that the only tool they have not utilized is charitable giving – philanthropy. Giving can get you a current income tax deduction and allows you to avoid capital gains tax. Giving will also reduce the amount of taxes your estate may owe when you leave this world and go home to live with the Lord.

I want all my donor clients to hear, "Well done, good and faithful servant." By following any of the strategies outlined in this book, you can significantly reduce your current income tax liability and advance your charitable giving – all at the same time.

As a result of reading this book, you the giver will not pay more in taxes than needed and can give more – much, much more – to the Kingdom.

> Matthew 22:21 – *"… He said to them, "Then give to Caesar the things that are Caesar's, and to God the things that are God's."*

CHAPTER 15

Summary of Strategies

THE FIRST TAKE-AWAY IS ONE that you already know, which is, *"In the beginning God created the heaven and the earth"* – Genesis 1:1. Everything in the world and everything you possess belongs to God. We are merely stewards or trustees of God's possessions. Someday, we all will have to give an accounting of how we managed God's possessions. The New Testament speaks more about wealth, money and possessions than any other topic – even heaven and hell combined. God is very concerned about your financial stewardship of His possessions! Thus, I have laid out financial tactics and strategies you can employ today and tomorrow in your stewardship journey.

Consider maximizing your charitable deduction. Remember, the IRS allows every taxpayer to deduct up to 50% of their AGI each year as a charitable contribution deduction. Your charitable contribution does not have to be all in cash. Your charitable contribution can be in the form of a business interest or other property. You may designate a beneficiary of an insurance policy or transfer the policy to a new owner.

GIFTING 5% OR 10% OWNERSHIP OF YOUR BUSINESS

You can lower your adjusted gross income (AGI) by gifting a business interest or some other type of real property to your

Donor Advised Fund (DAF) before a sale, or before you pass the business to the next generation. Gifting a share equal to 5-10% ownership of your business to a charity or your Donor Advised Fund would be the goal. By gifting this business interest or property to your DAF before a sale, you can avoid all capital gain tax on the sale. Even if you do not intend to sell your business or real property in the near future, consider the benefit of transferring *a portion of the business* interest to your DAF. You will receive a tax deduction for the value of the asset transferred in the year you establish the fund. You will enjoy additional income tax savings on the portion of income attributed to the DAF.

You can also avoid capital gains on highly appreciated common stock by gifting the stock to a DAF before the sale. Allow the sponsoring organization (e.g.: Waterstone, the National Christian Foundation, etc.) to sell the stock on behalf of the Donor Advised Fund.

If you need an immediate tax deduction within the current tax year but are not ready to set up a new private foundation or have not researched any charities for gifts, a DAF may be a good fit. The assets will remain in the DAF until you are ready to distribute those assets to worthy charities.

If you understand that giving can give you great personal satisfaction here on earth, but it can also help you hear, "Well done, good and faithful servant" when you're in your final home, this book has accomplished it mission.

Disclaimer
As stated elsewhere, local, national, or even global economic, tax, and general legal environments may at any time change not

only your personal circumstances, but the rules that you used to follow. Inform yourself of the status immediately before taking any action, simply to be sure that the environment and rules have not changed when you were not paying attention!

The information, general principles, and conclusions presented in this book are naturally my own, and may fall subject to local, territorial, state and federal laws and regulations, court cases and any revisions of same. While every care has been taken to give you practicable information in this book, I am really presenting only informational and educational background. This book should not be used as a substitute for the expert, informed and professional advice of an experienced attorney, accountant or other qualified professional.

Appendix A

Case Study: Donor Advised Fund

JACK AND KATHY SMITH'S ADJUSTED gross income (AGI) this year is projected to be $200,000. Their total net worth is $2 Million, including qualified retirement accounts and other investments.

The Smith's financial advisor warns them that if nothing changes, their total income tax bill for the current year will be about $57,000. He reminds them that if they wish to make additional charitable gifts of appreciated property, they can claim a charitable deduction of up to 30% of their adjusted gross income. So far this year, Jack and Kathy have given $10,000 of highly appreciated securities to their favorite charities. They could deduct up to $50,000 more in charitable gifts this year, but they are not sure which charities they would like to benefit with such significant current gift.

The Smiths decide to establish a Donor Advised Fund (DAF) and transfer into it $50,000 of securities that have doubled in value since they purchased them 10 years ago. Jack and Kathy select the name of their DAF and make recommendations for the selection of the investment advisor. Each year, they will make recommendations for the distributions that will be paid out of the DAF to public charities.

Jack and Kathy plan to use their Donor Advised Fund to help their children become more involved in and more aware of the pleasure and importance of charitable giving. They include their children in the decision making process, and allow them to make recommendations for a portion of the annual distributions to charities.

The $50,000 contribution to the Donor Advised Fund provides a $50,000 income tax deduction, and is projected to provide them current income tax savings of $19,000. Jack and Kathy also avoid $5,000 in state and federal capital gain taxes on the highly appreciated securities transferred to their Donor Advised Fund. Their total tax savings are $24,000.

I applied a marginal federal and state income tax rate of 38.25%, and a marginal federal and state capital gains tax rate of 19.25%. This example is hypothetical, to illustrate the potential solution only.

REFERENCES

Publications of Interest (The web links shown below were live at the time of publication of this book.)

- https://www.fidelitycharitable.org/docs/Using-Private-Foundations-and-Donor-Advised-Funds.pdf
- IRS Publication 526 – Charitable Contributions, https://www.irs.gov/pub/irs-pdf/p526.pdf
- "Incorporating Philanthropic Counsel into Your Advisory Practice" Kingdom Advisor's online training course by Jim Wise: https://kingdomadvisors.com/courses/incorporating-philanthropic-counsel-into-your-advisory-practice
- "The 2008 Study of High Net Worth – Issues Driving Charitable Activities among Affluent Households", March 2009, by the Center on Philanthropy at Indiana University, sponsored by Bank of America: http://newsroom.bankofamerica.com/files/press_kit/additional/2008_Study_of_High_Net_Worth_Philanthropy_03-01-2009.pdf
- www.smallfoundations.org
- "Family Wealth Counseling: Getting to the Heart of the Matter", by E.G. "Jay" Link & Jerry D. Nuerge, available at Financial Independence Group, http://www.finindgroup.com/products.htm
- "Investing in God's Business: The How-to of Smart Christian Giving", with Gregory L. Sperry and David H. Wills with Michael J. Dowling. Atlanta: The National Christian Foundation, 2005, also available at http://whatischarity.com/GG%20Library/library.generousgiving.org/paged03c.html?sec=74&page=390
- IRS reg. 1.170A-10: Charitable Contributions Carryovers of Individuals, https://www.law.cornell.edu/cfr/text/26/1.170A-10

- "Business Owners: Power of Giving", WaterStone publication, Kingdom Advisors, http://waterstone.org/resources/ebook-business-owners

WEBSITES OF INTEREST:

- www.sec.gov
- www.irs.gov
- www.kingdomadvisors.org
- https://www.onefpa.org
- http://www.nepsiscapital.com/
- www.waterstone.org
- www.nationalchristian.com
- www.giftplanning.com

ENDNOTES

i Read about nations' responses to the millennium's recession and attempts to stimulate their economies here: https://www.newyorkfed.org/medialibrary/media/research/current_issues/ci18-2.pdf and https://en.wikipedia.org/wiki/National_fiscal_policy_response_to_the_Great_Recession

ii You can read about Ramseyer's role and how the law unfolded here: http://digital.lib.uiowa.edu/bai/porter.htm

iii 75th Cong. Rec. 5906 (1932) (statement of Rep. Swing)

iv 75th Cong. Rec. 6159 (1932) (statement of Rep. Rankin, paraphrased): The decade of the Roaring 1920s had resulted in a distinctly **unequal distribution of wealth** in the country, and from 1921-28, the number of Americans with annual incomes over $1,000,000 increased from 21 to **511**, and those making between $500,000 and $1,000,000 annually increased from 63 to **983**. [Author Note: In **2016**, about 6% of Americans are earning over $200,000/year. There are about 6.4 million Americans earning more than $500,000/year and 10.4 million households earn over $1M/year.]

v Find the full speech text here: https://www.whitehouse.gov/the-press-office/2012/07/13/remarks-president-campaign-event-roanoke-virginia

vi 75th Cong. Rec. 5906 (1932) (statement of Rep. Swing, paraphrased): When the bubble burst and we entered economic depression, a populist backlash developed against the wealthiest Americans, their excess and their speculative investments. Proponents of increased taxation thus urged that the Revenue Act of 1932 should be designed not merely to raise revenue but should also "have for its purpose the **redistribution** of a part of these **tremendously large private fortunes**."

vii https://www.nolo.com/legal-encyclopedia/transfer-life-insurance-decrease-estate-tax-29585-2.html